Amazon WorkMail Administrator Guide

A catalogue record for this book is available from the Hong Kong Public Libraries.

Published in Hong Kong by Samurai Media Limited.

Email: info@samuraimedia.org

ISBN 9789888408580

Contents

What Is Amazon WorkMail?

Amazon WorkMail is a secure, managed business email and calendaring service with support for existing desktop and mobile email clients. You can access your email, contacts, and calendars using Microsoft Outlook, your browser, or their native iOS and Android email applications. You can integrate Amazon WorkMail with your existing corporate directory and control both the keys that encrypt your data and the location in which your data is stored.

Topics

- Amazon WorkMail Concepts
- Accessing Amazon WorkMail
- Amazon WorkMail Pricing
- Regions and Endpoints
- Amazon WorkMail Limits
- Related AWS Services
- Amazon WorkMail Resources

Amazon WorkMail Concepts

The terminology and concepts that are central to your understanding and use of Amazon WorkMail are described below.

Organization
A tenant setup for Amazon WorkMail.

Alias
A globally unique name to identify your organization. The alias is used to access the Amazon WorkMail web application (https://**youralias**.awsapps.com/mail).

Domain
The web address that comes after the @ symbol in an email address. You can add a domain that receives mail and delivers it to mailboxes in your organization.

Test mail domain
A domain is automatically configured during setup that can be used for testing Amazon WorkMail. The test mail domain is **youralias**.awsapps.com and is used as the default domain if you do not configure your own domain. The test mail domain is subject to different limits. For more information, see Amazon WorkMail Organization and User Limits.

Directory
An AWS Simple AD, AWS Managed AD, or AD Connector created in AWS Directory Service. If you create an organization using the Amazon WorkMail Quick setup, we create a WorkMail directory for you. You cannot view a WorkMail directory in AWS Directory Service.

User
A user created in the AWS Directory Service and enabled for Amazon WorkMail.

Group
A group used in AWS Directory Service used as distribution list or security group in Amazon WorkMail.

Mobile device policy
Various IT policy rules that control the security features and behavior of a mobile device.

Accessing Amazon WorkMail

Amazon WorkMail works with all major mobile devices and operating systems that support the Exchange ActiveSync protocol, including the Apple iPad, Apple iPhone, Amazon Kindle Fire, Android, Windows Phone, and BlackBerry 10.

You can access Amazon WorkMail from Microsoft Outlook on Windows. You must have a valid Microsoft Outlook license to use it with Amazon WorkMail, which offers native support for the following versions:

- Microsoft Outlook 2007, 2010, 2013, and 2016
- Microsoft Outlook 2010 and 2013 Click-to-Run
- Microsoft Outlook for Mac 2011
- Microsoft Outlook 2016 for Mac

Amazon WorkMail supports IMAP clients. For the required configuration, see Connect to your IMAP Client Application. POP3 clients are not currently supported.

You can access Amazon WorkMail using the web application: https://**alias**.awsapps.com/mail.

Amazon WorkMail Pricing

With Amazon WorkMail, there are no upfront fees or commitments. You pay only for active user accounts. For more specific information about pricing, see Pricing.

Regions and Endpoints

For a list of supported regions and endpoints, see AWS Regions and Endpoints.

Amazon WorkMail Limits

Amazon WorkMail can be used by enterprise customers as well as small business owners. Although we support most use cases without the need to configure any changes in limits, we also protect our users and the internet against abuse of the product. Therefore, some customers may run into limits that we have set. This section describes these limits and how to change them.

Some limit values can be changed, and some are hard limits that cannot be changed. If you want to change a limit value for Amazon WorkMail, follow these steps to submit a limit increase request:

1. Go to the AWS Support Center, sign in if prompted, and then choose **Create Case**.

2. Under **Regarding**, choose **Service Limit Increase**.

3. Under **Limit Type**, choose the type of limit to increase, fill in the necessary form fields, and then choose your preferred method of contact.

4. If you are requesting a limit increase for a specific organization, enter the **Organization Alias**.

5. Wait up to five working days for increases to become effective.

Note
It is possible to request a limit increase regardless of the age of the account. When you create a new AWS account, the values you are subjected to are usually lower than those for veteran accounts. On this page, only the default limit values for veteran accounts are listed.

Amazon WorkMail Organization and User Limits

You can add up to 25 users for a 30-day free trial. After this period ends, you are charged for all active users unless you remove them or close your Amazon WorkMail account.

All messages that are sent to another user are considered when evaluating these limits. These include emails, meeting requests, meeting responses, task requests, and messages that are forwarded or redirected automatically as the result of a rule.

Note
When requesting a limit increase request only for a specific organization, include the organization name in your request.

Resource	Default Limit	Upper Bound for Change Requests
Users per Amazon WorkMail organization	1,000	Can be increased depending on the directory type that is used for the organization: [See the AWS documentation website for more details] *If you are using Simple AD or AD Connector, see AWS Directory Service for additional information.
Free trial users	Up to 25 users in the first 30 days	The free trial period is only applicable for the first 25 users in any organization. Any additional users are not included in the free trial offer.
Recipients addressed per AWS account per day	100,000 recipients external to the organization, with no hard limit on recipients internal to the organization	There is no upper bound. However, Amazon WorkMail is a business email service and not intended to be used for bulk email services. For bulk email services, see Amazon SES or Amazon Pinpoint.
Recipients addressed per AWS account per day using any of the test domains	200 recipients, regardless of destination	There is no upper bound. However, the test mail domain is not intended for long-term usage. Instead, we recommend that you add your own domain and use it as the default domain.

WorkMail Organization Setting Limits

Resource	Default Limit
Number of domains per Amazon WorkMail organization	1,000 This is a hard limit and cannot be changed.
Number of sender patterns in email flow rules per organization	250 This is a hard limit and cannot be changed.

Per-User Limits

All messages that are sent to another user are considered when evaluating these limits. These include emails, meeting requests, meeting responses, task requests, and messages that are forwarded or redirected automatically as the result of a rule.

Resource	Default Limit	Upper Limit for Change Requests
Maximum size of mailbox	50 GB	50 GB
Maximum number of aliases per user	100 This is a hard limit and cannot be changed.	N/A
Recipients addressed per user per day using the domain that you own	10,000 recipients external to the organization, with no hard limit on recipients internal to the organization.	There is no upper bound. However, Amazon WorkMail is a business email service and not intended to be used for bulk email services. For bulk email services, see Amazon SES or Amazon Pinpoint.

Message Limits

All messages that are sent to another user are considered when evaluating these limits. These include emails, meeting requests, meeting responses, task requests, and messages that are forwarded or redirected automatically as the result of a rule.

Resource	Default Limit
Maximum size of incoming message	25 MBThis is a hard limit and cannot be changed.
Maximum size of outgoing message	25 MBThis is a hard limit and cannot be changed.
Number of recipients per message	500This is a hard limit and cannot be changed.

Related AWS Services

The following services are used along with Amazon WorkMail:

- **AWS Directory Service**—You can integrate Amazon WorkMail with an existing AWS Simple AD, AWS Managed AD, or AD Connector. Create a directory in the AWS Directory Service and then enable Amazon WorkMail for this directory. After you've configured this integration, you can choose which users you would like to enable for Amazon WorkMail from a list of users in your existing directory, and users can log in using their existing Active Directory credentials. For more information, see AWS Directory Service Administration Guide.

- **Amazon Simple Email Service**—Amazon WorkMail uses Amazon SES to send all outgoing email. The test mail domain and your domains are available for management in the Amazon SES console. There is no cost for outgoing email sent from Amazon WorkMail. For more information, see Amazon Simple Email Service Developer Guide.

- **AWS Identity and Access Management**—The AWS Management Console requires your user name and password so that any service you use can determine whether you have permission to access its resources. We recommend that you avoid using AWS account credentials to access AWS because AWS account credentials cannot be revoked or limited in any way. Instead, we recommend that you create an IAM user and add the user to an IAM group with administrative permissions. You can then access the console using the IAM user credentials.

If you signed up for AWS but have not created an IAM user for yourself, you can create one using the IAM console. For more information, see Create Individual IAM Users in the *IAM User Guide*.

- **AWS Key Management Service**—Amazon WorkMail is integrated with AWS KMS for encryption of customer data. Key management can be performed from the AWS KMS console. For more information, see What is the AWS Key Management Service in the *AWS Key Management Service Developer Guide*.

Amazon WorkMail Resources

The following related resources can help you as you work with this service.

- ** Classes & Workshops** – Links to role-based and specialty courses as well as self-paced labs to help sharpen your AWS skills and gain practical experience.
- ** AWS Developer Tools** – Links to developer tools, SDKs, IDE toolkits, and command line tools for developing and managing AWS applications.
- ** AWS Whitepapers** – Links to a comprehensive list of technical AWS whitepapers, covering topics such as architecture, security, and economics and authored by AWS Solutions Architects or other technical experts.
- ** AWS Support Center** – The hub for creating and managing your AWS Support cases. Also includes links to other helpful resources, such as forums, technical FAQs, service health status, and AWS Trusted Advisor.
- ** AWS Support** – The primary web page for information about AWS Support, a one-on-one, fast-response support channel to help you build and run applications in the cloud.
- ** Contact Us** – A central contact point for inquiries concerning AWS billing, account, events, abuse, and other issues.
- ** AWS Site Terms** – Detailed information about our copyright and trademark; your account, license, and site access; and other topics.

Getting Set Up

To use Amazon WorkMail you'll need an AWS account. If you haven't signed up for AWS yet, complete the following tasks to get set up.

Topics

- Get an AWS Account and Your AWS Credentials
- Sign in to the Amazon WorkMail Console
- AWS Identity and Access Management Users and Groups

Get an AWS Account and Your AWS Credentials

To access AWS, you will need to sign up for an AWS account.

To sign up for an AWS account

1. Open https://aws.amazon.com/, and then choose **Create an AWS Account**. **Note**
   This might be unavailable in your browser if you previously signed into the AWS Management Console. In that case, choose **Sign in to a different account**, and then choose **Create a new AWS account**.

2. Follow the online instructions.

   Part of the sign-up procedure involves receiving a phone call and entering a PIN using the phone keypad.

AWS sends you a confirmation e-mail after the sign-up process is complete. At any time, you can view your current account activity and manage your account by going to https://aws.amazon.com/ and clicking **My Account/Console**.

To get the access key ID and secret access key for an IAM user

Access keys consist of an access key ID and secret access key, which are used to sign programmatic requests that you make to AWS. If you don't have access keys, you can create them from the AWS Management Console. We recommend that you use IAM access keys instead of AWS account root user access keys. IAM lets you securely control access to AWS services and resources in your AWS account.

The only time that you can view or download the secret access keys is when you create the keys. You cannot recover them later. However, you can create new access keys at any time. You must also have permissions to perform the required IAM actions. For more information, see Permissions Required to Access IAM Resources in the *IAM User Guide*.

1. Open the IAM console.

2. In the navigation pane of the console, choose **Users**.

3. Choose your IAM user name (not the check box).

4. Choose the **Security credentials** tab and then choose **Create access key**.

5. To see the new access key, choose **Show**. Your credentials will look something like this:

   - Access key ID: AKIAIOSFODNN7EXAMPLE
   - Secret access key: wJalrXUtnFEMI/K7MDENG/bPxRfiCYEXAMPLEKEY

6. To download the key pair, choose **Download .csv file**. Store the keys in a secure location.

   Keep the keys confidential in order to protect your AWS account, and never email them. Do not share them outside your organization, even if an inquiry appears to come from AWS or Amazon.com. No one who legitimately represents Amazon will ever ask you for your secret key.

Related topics

- What Is IAM? in the *IAM User Guide*

- AWS Security Credentials in *AWS General Reference*

Sign in to the Amazon WorkMail Console

You must sign in to the Amazon WorkMail console before you can add users and manage accounts and mailboxes.

To sign in to the Amazon WorkMail console

1. Sign in to the AWS Management Console and open the Amazon WorkMail console at https://console.aws.amazon.com/workmail/.

2. If necessary, change the region. From the navigation bar, select the region that meets your needs. For more information, see Regions and Endpoints in the *Amazon Web Services General Reference*.

AWS Identity and Access Management Users and Groups

The AWS Management Console requires your username and password so that the service can determine whether you have permission to access its resources. We recommend that you avoid using root account credentials to access AWS because root account credentials cannot be revoked or limited in any way. Instead, use AWS Identity and Access Management (IAM) to create an IAM user and add the user to an IAM group with administrative permissions. You can then access the console using the credentials for the IAM user.

If you signed up for AWS but have not created an IAM user for yourself, you can create one using the IAM console. For more information, see Create Individual IAM Users in *IAM User Guide*.

AWS Identity and Access Management Policies for Amazon WorkMail

By default, IAM users don't have permissions to manage Amazon WorkMail resources; you must attach an AWS managed policy (**AmazonWorkMailFullAccess** or **AmazonWorkMailReadOnlyAccess**) or create a customer managed policy that explicitly grants IAM users those permissions, and attach the policy to the specific IAM users or groups that require those permissions. For more information, see Managing Managed Policies Using the AWS Management Console in *IAM User Guide*. For more information, see Permissions and Policies in *IAM User Guide*.

The following customer managed policy statement grants an IAM user full access to Amazon WorkMail resources. This customer managed policy gives the same level of access as the AWS managed policy **AmazonWorkMail-FullAccess**. Either policy gives the user access to all Amazon WorkMail, AWS Key Management Service, Amazon Simple Email Service, and AWS Directory Service operations, as well as several Amazon EC2 operations that Amazon WorkMail needs to be able to perform on your behalf.

```
1  "amazonWorkMailFullAccess": {
2    "name": "Amazon WorkMail Full Access",
3    "description": "Provides full access to WorkMail, Directory Service, SES, EC2 and read access
        to KMS metadata.",
4    "policyDocument": {
5        "Version": "2012-10-17",
6        "Statement": [
7                    {
8                        "Effect": "Allow",
9                        "Action": [
10                            "workmail:*",
11                            "ds:AuthorizeApplication",
12                            "ds:CheckAlias",
13                            "ds:CreateAlias",
14                            "ds:CreateDirectory",
15                            "ds:CreateDomain",
16                            "ds:DeleteAlias",
17                            "ds:DeleteDirectory",
18                            "ds:DescribeDirectories",
19                            "ds:ExtendDirectory",
20                            "ds:GetDirectoryLimits",
21                            "ds:ListAuthorizedApplications",
22                            "ds:UnauthorizeApplication",
23                            "ses:*",
24                            "ec2:AuthorizeSecurityGroupEgress",
25                            "ec2:AuthorizeSecurityGroupIngress",
26                            "ec2:CreateNetworkInterface",
27                            "ec2:CreateSecurityGroup",
28                            "ec2:DeleteSecurityGroup",
```

```
29                    "ec2:CreateSubnet",
30                    "ec2:DeleteSubnet",
31                    "ec2:CreateVpc",
32                    "ec2:DeleteVpc",
33                    "ec2:DescribeRouteTables",
34                    "ec2:DescribeSubnets",
35                    "ec2:DescribeVpcs",
36                    "ec2:DescribeAvailabilityZones",
37                    "ec2:CreateTags",
38                    "ec2:RevokeSecurityGroupEgress",
39                    "ec2:RevokeSecurityGroupIngress",
40                    "kms:DescribeKey",
41                    "kms:ListAliases"
42                    ],
43                "Resource": "*"
44            }
45        ]
46    }
47 }
```

The following customer managed policy statement grants an IAM user read-only access to Amazon WorkMail resources. This customer managed policy gives the same level of access as the AWS managed policy **AmazonWorkMailReadOnlyAccess**. Either policy gives the user access to all of the Amazon WorkMail Describe operations. Access to the two Amazon EC2 operations are necessary so Amazon WorkMail can obtain a list of your VPCs and subnets. Access to the AWS Directory Service `DescribeDirectories` operation is needed to obtain information about your AWS Directory Service directories. Access to the Amazon SES service is needed to obtain information about the configured domains and access to AWS Key Management Service is needed to obtain information about the used encryption keys.

```
1 "amazonWorkMailROAccess": {
2   "name": "Amazon WorkMail Read Only Access",
3   "description": "Provides read only access to WorkMail and SES.",
4   "policyDocument": {
5       "Version": "2012-10-17",
6       "Statement": [
7                   {
8                       "Effect": "Allow",
9                       "Action": [
10                          "workmail:Get*",
11                          "workmail:List*",
12                          "workmail:Describe*",
13                          "workmail:Search*",
14                          "ses:Get*",
15                          "ses:Describe*"
16                          ],
17                      "Resource": "*"
18                  }
19              ]
20    }
21 }
```

Getting Started With Amazon WorkMail

Whether you are a new Amazon WorkMail user or an existing user of Amazon WorkDocs or Amazon WorkSpaces, you can get started with Amazon WorkMail by completing the following steps.

1. After you log in to your AWS account, the first step is set up your organization. For more information, see Add an Organization.

2. After successfully adding your organization, you can add your domain to Amazon WorkMail. For more information, see Add a Domain.

3. Create new users or enable your existing directory users for Amazon WorkMail. For more information, see Create New Users.

4. Migrate your existing Microsoft Exchange mailboxes to Amazon WorkMail. For more information, see Migrating to Amazon WorkMail.

5. To use Amazon WorkMail from your existing desktop client, set up your Microsoft Outlook client. For more information, see Connect Microsoft Outlook to Your Amazon WorkMail Account.

6. To use Amazon WorkMail from anywhere on a mobile device, set up Amazon WorkMail on your Kindle, Android, iPad, iPhone, or Windows Phone. For more information, see Connect Your iOS Device and Connect Your Android Device.

7. To use Amazon WorkMail with any IMAP-compatible client software, see Connect IMAP Clients to Your Amazon WorkMail Account.

Working with Organizations

In Amazon WorkMail, your organization represents the users in your company. In the Amazon WorkMail console, you see a list of your available organizations. If you don't have any available, you must create one in order to use Amazon WorkMail. After you create an organization, it can have one of the following states.

State	Description
Active	Your organization is healthy and ready for use.
Creating	A workflow is running to create your organization.
Failed	Your organization could not be created.
Impaired	Your organization is malfunctioning or an issue has been detected.
Inactive	Your organization is inactive.
Requested	Your organization creation request is in the queue and waiting to be created.
Validating	All settings for the organization are being health-checked.

Topics

- Add an Organization
- Remove an Organization
- Edit Your Organization's Mobile Device Policy

Add an Organization

To use Amazon WorkMail, you must first add an organization. One AWS account can have multiple Amazon WorkMail organizations. You can then add users, groups, and domains.

The following setup options are available:

- **Quick setup**: Get started with Amazon WorkMail in 2 minutes. For more information, see Set up Amazon WorkMail with Quick Setup.
- **Standard setup**: Integrate Amazon WorkMail with an existing directory such as an on-premises Microsoft Active Directory, AWS Managed Active Directory, or AWS Simple Active Directory. For more information, see Integrate Amazon WorkMail with an Existing Directory (Standard Setup).

Set up Amazon WorkMail with Quick Setup

Use the Quick setup to get an Amazon WorkMail organization in 2 minutes. Amazon WorkMail does the following for you:

- Creates a new WorkMail Directory for storing your users and groups. You cannot view this type of directory in AWS Directory Service.
- Creates a free test domain.
- Uses the default KMS master key for encrypting your mailbox contents.

To add an organization using the Quick setup option

1. Open the Amazon WorkMail console at https://console.aws.amazon.com/workmail/.

2. In the navigation bar, select the region that meets your needs. For more information, see Regions and Endpoints in the *Amazon Web Services General Reference*.

3. Choose **Get started**.

4. On the **Set up your organization** screen, choose **Quick setup**.

5. On the **Quick setup** screen, for **Organization name**, enter a unique alias to be used as your mail domain, and then choose **Create**.

   After your organization is created, you can add domains, users, and groups. **Note**
   If you exceed the number of organizations you can create using the Quick setup, you receive the error 'You have reached the maximum number of organizations you can create'. For more information, see Amazon WorkMail Limits.

Integrate Amazon WorkMail with an Existing Directory (Standard Setup)

You can integrate Amazon WorkMail with an existing directory such as an on-premises Microsoft Active Directory, AWS Managed Active Directory, or AWS Simple Active Directory. By integrating with your on-premises directory, you can reuse your existing users and groups in Amazon WorkMail and users can log in with their existing credentials.

You also have the option to select a specific master key that Amazon WorkMail uses to encrypt the mailbox content. You can either select the default master key for Amazon WorkMail or create a custom master key in AWS KMS to use with Amazon WorkMail.

If the existing directory is on-premises, you must first set up an AD Connector in AWS Directory Service. The AD Connector is used to synchronize your users and groups to the Amazon WorkMail address book and perform user authentication requests.

For information about setting up an AD Connector, see Connecting to Your Existing Directory with AD Connector in the *AWS Directory Service Administration Guide*.

To perform a Standard setup

1. Open the Amazon WorkMail console at https://console.aws.amazon.com/workmail/.

2. In the navigation bar, select the region that meets your needs. For more information, see Regions and Endpoints in the *Amazon Web Services General Reference*.

3. Choose **Get started**.

4. On the **Set up your organization** screen, choose **Standard setup**.

5. On the **Standard setup** screen, for **Available Directories**, select your existing directory. **Note**
   If you have an on-premises Active Directory with Microsoft Exchange and an AWS AD Connector, choose **Enable interoperability** on the **Interoperability with Microsoft Exchange** screen. Interoperability allows you to minimize disruption to your users as you migrate mailboxes to Amazon WorkMail, or use Amazon WorkMail for a subset of your corporate mailboxes. For more information, see Interoperability between Amazon WorkMail and Microsoft Exchange.

6. For **Master keys**, select a master key. You can either select the default master key or create a custom master key in AWS Key Management Service. **Note**
   For information about creating a new master key, see Creating Keys in the *AWS Key Management Service Developer Guide*.
   If you are logged on as an IAM user, make yourself a key administrator on the master key. For more information, see Enabling and Disabling Keys in the *AWS Key Management Service Developer Guide*.

Remove an Organization

If you no longer want to use Amazon WorkMail for your organization's email, you can delete your organization from Amazon WorkMail.

Note
This operation cannot be undone, and you will not be able to recover your mailbox data.

To remove an organization

1. Open the Amazon WorkMail console at https://console.aws.amazon.com/workmail/.

2. If necessary, change the region. From the navigation bar, select the region that meets your needs. For more information, see Regions and Endpoints in the *Amazon Web Services General Reference*.

3. On the **Organizations** screen, in the list of organizations, select the organization to remove and choose **Remove**.

4. For **Remove organization**, enter the name of the organization, and then choose whether to keep the existing user directory or delete it.

5. Choose **Remove** to save these changes.

Note
If you didn't provide your own directory for Amazon WorkMail, then we created one for you. If you keep this existing directory when you remove the organization, you will be charged for it unless it is being used by Amazon WorkMail, Amazon WorkDocs, or Amazon WorkSpaces. For pricing information, see Other Directory Types Pricing.
To delete the directory, it cannot have any other AWS applications enabled. For more information, see Deleting a Simple AD Directory or Deleting an AD Connector Directory in the *AWS Directory Service Administration Guide*.

Edit Your Organization's Mobile Device Policy

You can edit your organization's mobile device policy to change the way that mobile devices interact with Amazon WorkMail.

To edit your organization's mobile device policy

1. Open the Amazon WorkMail console at https://console.aws.amazon.com/workmail/.

2. If necessary, change the region. From the navigation bar, select the region that meets your needs. For more information, see Regions and Endpoints in the *Amazon Web Services General Reference*.

3. On the **Organizations** screen, in the **Alias** column, select the organization to edit.

4. In the navigation pane, choose **Mobile Policies**, and then on the **Default mobile policy** screen, choose **Edit**.

5. Update any of the following as necessary:

    1. **Password required**: Require a password to lock a mobile device.

    2. **Allow simple password**: Use the PIN on the device as the password.

    3. **Minimal password length**: Set the number of characters required in a valid password.

    4. **Require alphanumeric password**: Require that passwords are made up of letters and numbers.

    5. **Minimum number of character sets**: Specify the number of character sets required in a password, such as lowercase and uppercase letters, symbols, and numbers.

    6. **Number of failed attempts allowed**: Specify the number of failed login attempts that are allowed before the user is locked out of their account.

    7. **Password expiration**: Specify the number of days before a password expires and must be changed.

    8. **Enable screen lock**: Specify the number of seconds that must elapse without user input to lock the user's screen.

    9. **Enforce password history**: Specify the number of passwords that can be entered before repeating the same password.

    10. **Require encryption on device**: Encrypt email data on the mobile device.

    11. **Require encryption on storage card**: Encrypt email data on the mobile device's removable storage.

6. Choose **Save**.

Working with Users

You can create and remove users from Amazon WorkMail. In addition, you can reset their email passwords and wipe the data from their mobile devices.

Topics

- Create New Users
- Edit User Email Addresses
- Enable Existing Users
- Edit User Details
- Reset User Passwords
- Disable User Mailboxes
- Restore Disabled Mailboxes
- Remotely Wipe Mobile Devices
- Remove a User's Mobile Devices from the Devices List
- View Mobile Device Details
- Enable Signed or Encrypted Email

Create New Users

When you create new users, Amazon WorkMail creates mailboxes for them. Users can log in and access their mail from the Amazon WorkMail web application, mobile device, or Microsoft Outlook on macOS or PC.

To create a new user

1. Open the Amazon WorkMail console at https://console.aws.amazon.com/workmail/.

2. If necessary, change the region. From the navigation bar, select the region that meets your needs. For more information, see Regions and Endpoints in the *Amazon Web Services General Reference*.

3. On the **Organizations** screen, in the list of organizations, select your organization's alias.

4. In the navigation pane on the left, choose **Users** to see a list of all users in the directory, including enabled, disabled, and system users.

5. To create a new user, choose **Create User**.

6. On the **Add the details for your new user** screen, enter the user's first and last name, username, and display name and then choose **Next**.

7. On the **Set up email address and password** screen, enter the user's email address and password, and choose **Add user**.

Edit User Email Addresses

You can assign multiple email addresses to a single user and the default email address is used as the default sending address for outgoing email.

You can also add one or more email aliases, which can be used to send or receive email from a different address or domain. For more information, see Send as an Alias.

To edit a user's email address

1. Open the Amazon WorkMail console at https://console.aws.amazon.com/workmail/.

2. If necessary, change the region. From the navigation bar, select the region that meets your needs. For more information, see Regions and Endpoints in the *Amazon Web Services General Reference*.

3. On the **Organizations** screen, in the list of organizations, select your organization's alias.

4. In the navigation pane, choose **Users**, and then in the list of users, select the name of the user to edit.

5. On the **General** tab, choose **Edit**, **Add email address**, and then type the email address to add to this user.

6. To set the new email address as the default, choose **Set as default**.

Enable Existing Users

When Amazon WorkMail is integrated with your corporate Active Directory or you already have users available in your Simple AD directory, you can enable these users in Amazon WorkMail.

To enable an existing directory user

1. Open the Amazon WorkMail console at https://console.aws.amazon.com/workmail/.

2. If necessary, change the region. From the navigation bar, select the region that meets your needs. For more information, see Regions and Endpoints in the *Amazon Web Services General Reference*.

3. On the **Organizations** screen, in the list of organizations, select your organization's alias.

4. In the navigation pane, choose **Users** to see a list of all the users in the directory, including enabled, disabled, and system users.

5. From the list of disabled users, select the users to enable and choose **Enable user**.

6. In the **Enable user(s)** dialog box, review the primary email address and choose **Enable**.

Edit User Details

You can edit a user's first and last name, email address, display name, address, phone number, and company details.

Note
If you are integrating Amazon WorkMail with an AD Connector directory, you can't edit these details from the AWS Management Console. Instead, you must edit them using your Active Directory management tools.

To edit a user's details

1. Open the Amazon WorkMail console at https://console.aws.amazon.com/workmail/.

2. If necessary, change the region. From the navigation bar, select the region that meets your needs. For more information, see Regions and Endpoints in the *Amazon Web Services General Reference*.

3. On the **Organizations** screen, in the list of organizations, select your organization's alias.

4. In the navigation pane, choose **Users** and select the name of the user to edit.

5. On the **General** tab, choose **Edit**, and then update any of the fields as appropriate.

Reset User Passwords

If a user forgets a password or is having trouble signing in to Amazon WorkMail, you can reset the password. If you are integrating Amazon WorkMail with an AD Connector directory, you have to reset the user password in Active Directory.

To reset a user password

1. Open the Amazon WorkMail console at https://console.aws.amazon.com/workmail/.

2. If necessary, change the region. From the navigation bar, select the region that meets your needs. For more information, see Regions and Endpoints in the *Amazon Web Services General Reference*.

3. On the **Organizations** screen, in the list of organizations, select your organization's alias.

4. In the navigation pane, choose **Users**.

5. In the list of users, select the name of the user to edit and choose **Reset password**.

6. In the **Reset Password** dialog box, type the new password and choose **Reset**. **Note**
   Amazon WorkMail enforces password policies, but additional policies may be applicable. If the attempt to reset the password is unsuccessful, verify any password policies that are set in the directory.

Disable User Mailboxes

You can disable user mailboxes when they are no longer needed. Amazon WorkMail keeps mailboxes for 30 days before they're permanently removed.

To disable a user's mailbox

1. Open the Amazon WorkMail console at https://console.aws.amazon.com/workmail/.

2. If necessary, change the region. From the navigation bar, select the region that meets your needs. For more information, see Regions and Endpoints in the *Amazon Web Services General Reference*.

3. On the **Organizations** screen, in the list of organizations, select your organization's alias.

4. In the navigation pane, select **Users**, select the name of the user to disable, and choose **Disable User**.

5. In the **Disable user(s)** dialog box, choose **Disable**.

Restore Disabled Mailboxes

Amazon WorkMail retains disabled mailboxes for 30 days before permanently removing them. To restore a mailbox, use the same steps as enabling an existing user.

Important

Mailboxes cannot be restored if the organization containing them has been deleted. To restore a user's disabled mailbox, the user must be still in the directory. If the user isn't in the directory or if you've re-created them, the mailbox cannot be restored because each mailbox is linked to a unique user ID.

To restore a deleted mailbox

1. Open the Amazon WorkMail console at https://console.aws.amazon.com/workmail/.

2. If necessary, change the region. From the navigation bar, select the region that meets your needs. For more information, see Regions and Endpoints in the *Amazon Web Services General Reference*.

3. On the **Organizations** screen, in the list of organizations, select your organization's alias.

4. In the navigation pane, choose **Users** to see a list of enabled, disabled, and system users.

5. From the list of disabled users, select the users to enable and choose **Enable user**.

6. In the **Enable user(s)** dialog box, review the primary email address of the user and choose **Enable**.

Remotely Wipe Mobile Devices

You can only remotely wipe user devices when they are connected to Amazon WorkMail. If a device is disconnected from the network, this procedure doesn't work.

Warning
For most mobile devices, a remote wipe resets the device to factory defaults. All data, including personal files, can be removed when you perform this procedure.

To remotely wipe a user's mobile device

1. Open the Amazon WorkMail console at https://console.aws.amazon.com/workmail/.

2. If necessary, change the region. From the navigation bar, select the region that meets your needs. For more information, see Regions and Endpoints in the *Amazon Web Services General Reference*.

3. On the **Organizations** screen, in the list of organizations, select your organization's alias.

4. In the navigation pane, choose **Users**, select the user with the device to view, and choose **Mobile**.

5. In the list of devices, select the device to wipe and choose **Wipe device**.

6. Check the status in overview to see whether the wipe is requested.

7. After the device is wiped, you can remove the device from the list. **Important**
   To re-add a device, make sure the device is removed from the list; otherwise, the device will be wiped again.

Remove a User's Mobile Devices from the Devices List

If a user is no longer using a certain mobile device or the device is remote wiped, you can remove it from the list. When the user configures the device again, it shows up in the list.

To remove a user's mobile devices from the devices list

1. Open the Amazon WorkMail console at https://console.aws.amazon.com/workmail/.

2. If necessary, change the region. From the navigation bar, select the region that meets your needs. For more information, see Regions and Endpoints in the *Amazon Web Services General Reference*.

3. On the **Organizations** screen, in the list of organizations, select your organization's alias.

4. In the navigation pane, choose **Users**, select the user with the device to view, and choose **Mobile**.

5. In the list of devices, select the device to remove and choose **Remove device**.

View Mobile Device Details

You can view the details of a user's mobile device.

Note

Some devices don't send all of their details to the server, so you may not see all available device details.

To view device details

1. Open the Amazon WorkMail console at https://console.aws.amazon.com/workmail/.

2. If necessary, change the region. From the navigation bar, select the region that meets your needs. For more information, see Regions and Endpoints in the *Amazon Web Services General Reference.*

3. On the **Organizations** screen, in the list of organizations, select your organization's alias.

4. In the navigation pane, choose **Users**, select the user with device to view, and choose **Mobile**.

5. In the list of devices, select the device whose details you want to view. Device status codes are listed in the following table.
[See the AWS documentation website for more details]

Enable Signed or Encrypted Email

You can use S/MIME to enable users to send signed or encrypted email both inside and outside the organization.

Note
User certificates in the Global Address List (GAL) are supported only in a connected Active Directory setup.

To enable users to send signed or encrypted emails

1. Set up an Active Directory (AD) Connector. Setting up an AD Connector with your on-premises directory allows users to continue to use their existing corporate credentials.

2. Configure Certificate Autoenrollment to issue and store user certificates automatically in the Active Directory. Amazon WorkMail receives user certificates from the Active Directory and publishes them to the GAL. For more information, see Configure Certificate Autoenrollment.

3. Distribute the generated certificates to users by exporting the certificates from the exchange server and mailing them.

4. Each user installs the certificate to their email program (such as Windows Outlook) and mobile devices.

Working with Groups

Groups can be used as distribution lists in Amazon WorkMail for receiving emails for generic email addresses like sales@example.com or support@example.com. You can also use them as security groups to share a mailbox or calendar with a certain team. It can take up to 2 hours before newly added groups appear in your Microsoft Outlook offline address book.

Topics

- Create a Group
- Enable an Existing Group
- Disable a Group

Create a Group

To create a group

1. Open the Amazon WorkMail console at https://console.aws.amazon.com/workmail/.

2. If necessary, change the region. From the navigation bar, select the region that meets your needs. For more information, see Regions and Endpoints in the *Amazon Web Services General Reference.*

3. On the **Organizations** screen, in the **Alias** column, select the name of the organization to which to add a group.

4. In the navigation pane, choose **Groups** to see a list of enabled, disabled, and system groups.

5. To create a new group, choose **Create group**.

6. On the **Add group details** screen, enter the group name and email address, and then choose **Add group members**.

7. On the **Add members to group** screen, for **Search**, enter the user's first name, last name, user name, or group name and press **Enter**.

8. In the list of directory users and groups, select the user or groups to add as a member.

9. Choose the right arrow button to add them to the list of selected users/groups and then choose **Finish**.

Enable an Existing Group

When Amazon WorkMail is integrated with your corporate Active Directory or you already have groups available in your Simple AD directory, you can use these groups as security groups or distribution lists in Amazon WorkMail.

To enable an existing directory group

1. Open the Amazon WorkMail console at https://console.aws.amazon.com/workmail/.

2. If necessary, change the region. From the navigation bar, select the region that meets your needs. For more information, see Regions and Endpoints in the *Amazon Web Services General Reference*.

3. On the **Organizations** screen, in the **Alias** column, select the name of the organization to which to add a group.

4. In the navigation pane, choose **Groups** to see a list of enabled, disabled, and system groups.

5. From the list of disabled groups, select the groups to enable and choose **Enable Group**.

6. In the **Enable group(s)** dialog box, review the primary email address and choose **Enable**.

Disable a Group

When you no longer need a group, you can disable it.

To disable a group

1. Open the Amazon WorkMail console at https://console.aws.amazon.com/workmail/.

2. If necessary, change the region. From the navigation bar, select the region that meets your needs. For more information, see Regions and Endpoints in the *Amazon Web Services General Reference*.

3. On the **Organizations** screen, in the **Alias** column, select the name of the organization from which to remove a group.

4. In the navigation pane, choose **Groups**.

5. In the list of groups, select the group to disable, and then choose **Disable group**.

6. In the **Disable group(s)** dialog box, choose **Disable**.

Working with Mailbox Permissions

You can use mailbox permissions in Amazon WorkMail to grant users or groups the right to work in other users' mailboxes. Mailbox permissions apply to an entire mailbox, enabling multiple users to access the same mailbox without sharing the credentials for that mailbox. Users with mailbox permissions can read and modify mailbox data and send email from the shared mailbox.

The following list shows the permissions that you can grant:

- **Send On Behalf**: Enables a user or group to send email on behalf of another user. The mailbox owner appears in the **From:** header, and the sender appears in the **Sender:** header.
- **Send As**: Enables a user or group to send email as the mailbox owner, without showing the actual sender of the message. The mailbox owner appears in both the **From:** and **Sender:** headers.
- **Full Access**: Enables full read and write access to the mailbox, including permissions to modify folder-level permissions.

Note
Granting mailbox permissions to a group extends those permissions to all the members of that group, including members of nested groups.

When you grant mailbox permissions, the Amazon WorkMail AutoDiscover service automatically updates access to those mailboxes for the users or groups you added.

For the Microsoft Outlook client in Windows, users with full access permissions can automatically access the shared mailboxes. Allow up to 60 minutes for the changes to propagate, or restart Microsoft Outlook.

For the Amazon WorkMail web application and other email clients, users with full access permissions can manually open the shared mailboxes. Opened mailboxes stay open, even between sessions, unless the user closes them.

Topics

- Mailbox and Folder Permissions
- Enabling Mailbox Permissions
- Editing Mailbox Permissions
- Removing Mailbox Permissions
- Managing Group Permissions

Mailbox and Folder Permissions

Mailbox permissions apply to all folders in a mailbox. These permissions can only be enabled by the AWS account holder or the IAM user authorized to call the Amazon WorkMail management API. To apply the permissions to mailboxes or groups as a whole, log in to the AWS Management Console or use the Amazon WorkMail API.

Folder permissions apply only to a single folder. These permissions can be set by end users, either by using an email client or by using the Amazon WorkMail web application.

Enabling Mailbox Permissions

You can enable other users to access a mailbox using the Amazon WorkMail web application.

To enable mailbox permissions

1. In the Amazon WorkMail application, on the **User details** page under **Permissions**, choose **Add or remove**.

2. Under **Users and groups**, select the user or group to share your inbox and choose » to add them to the **Permissions** list. Choose **Save**.

3. On the **Permissions** tab, select the level of permissions to grant and choose **Save**.

Updated permissions can take up to five minutes to propagate.

Editing Mailbox Permissions

You can edit existing mailbox permissions for Amazon WorkMail.

To edit mailbox permissions

1. In the Amazon WorkMail application, on the **User details** page under **Permissions**, choose **Edit**.

2. Select the permissions to change and choose **Save**.

Updated permissions can take up to five minutes to propagate.

Removing Mailbox Permissions

You can remove existing mailbox permissions for Amazon WorkMail.

To remove mailbox permissions

1. In the Amazon WorkMail application, on the **User details** page under **Permissions**, choose **Add or remove**.

2. Under **Users and groups**, select the user or group and remove them from the **Permissions** list.

3. Choose **Save**.

Updated permissions can take up to five minutes to propagate.

Managing Group Permissions

You can add or remove group permissions for Amazon WorkMail.

Note
Full Access permissions are not available for groups, because groups do not have a mailbox to access.

To manage group permissions

1. In the Amazon WorkMail application, on the **Groups** page under **WorkMail groups**, select the group to manage.

2. Under **Permissions**, choose **Add or remove**.

3. Under **Users and groups**, select the group to add or remove. Add or remove them from the **Permissions** list and choose **Save**. **Note**
If you added a group to the **Permissions** list, select the level of permissions to grant under the **Permissions** tab and choose **Save**.

Updated permissions can take up to five minutes to propagate.

Working with Domains

You can add or remove email domains or make them the default.

Topics

- Add a Domain
- Remove a Domain
- Choose the Default Domain
- Verify Domains
- Edit Domain Identity Policies
- Authenticate Email with SPF

Add a Domain

You can add up to 100 domains to your organization. When you add a new domain, an Amazon SES sending authorization policy is automatically added to the domain identity policy. This provides Amazon WorkMail with access to all Amazon SES sending actions for your domain and allows you to redirect email to your domain as well as external domains.

Important
Some DNS providers automatically append the domain name to the end of DNS records. Adding a record that already contains the domain name (such as _amazonses.example.com) might result in the duplication of the domain name (such as _amazonses.example.com.example.com). To avoid duplication of the domain name, add a period to the end of the domain name in the DNS record. This will indicate to your DNS provider that the record name is fully qualified (that is, no longer relative to the domain name), and prevent the DNS provider from appending an additional domain name.

Note
As a best practice, you should add aliases for postmaster@ and abuse@. You can create distribution groups for these aliases if you want certain users in your organization to receive mail sent to these aliases.

To add a domain

1. Sign in to the AWS Management Console and open the Amazon WorkMail console at https://console.aws.amazon.com/workmail/.

2. If necessary, change the region. From the navigation bar, select the region that meets your needs. For more information, see Regions and Endpoints in the *Amazon Web Services General Reference*.

3. On the **Organizations** screen, in the **Alias** column, select the name of the organization to which to add a domain.

4. In the navigation pane, choose **Domains**, **Add domain**.

5. On the **Add domain** screen, enter the domain name to add,and choose **Add domain**.

6. On the next screen, in the **Step 1: verify domain ownership** section, the TXT record verifies your ownership of the domain.

   After all your users and distribution groups are created, and mailboxes are successfully migrated, you can switch the MX record to start delivering email to Amazon WorkMail. Updates to the DNS record can take up to 72 hours to be processed and made active, however updates are often processed and made active sooner than this.

7. In the **Step 2: Finalize domain setup** section, the following records are listed:

   - The MX record to deliver incoming email to Amazon WorkMail.
   - The CNAME autodiscover record that allows users to easily configure their Microsoft Outlook or mobile device knowing only their email address and password.
   - The CNAME records for DKIM signing. For more information about DKIM signing, see Authenticating Email with DKIM in the *Amazon Simple Email Service Developer Guide*.

   We recommend that you set the Time to Live (TTL) to 3600 of the MX and autodiscover CNAME record. Reducing the TTL ensures that your mail servers don't use outdated or invalid MX records after updating your MX records or migrating your mailboxes.

   For more information about adding these DNS records to Amazon Route 53, see Routing Queries to Amazon WorkMail (Public Hosted Zones Only) in the *Amazon Route 53 Developer Guide*.

Remove a Domain

When you no longer need a domain, you can delete it.

Note
You can't delete a domain when there are users or groups using the domain as their email address.

To remove a domain

1. Sign in to the AWS Management Console and open the Amazon WorkMail console at https://console.aws. amazon.com/workmail/.

2. If necessary, change the region. From the navigation bar, select the region that meets your needs. For more information, see Regions and Endpoints in the *Amazon Web Services General Reference*.

3. On the **Organizations** screen, in the **Alias** column, select the name of the organization from which to remove the domain.

4. In the list of domains, select the check box next to the domain name and choose **Remove**.

5. In the **Remove domain** dialog box, type the name of the domain to remove and choose **Remove**.

Choose the Default Domain

To use a domain as default in the email address of your users and groups, you can choose a default domain. Making a domain the default does not change existing email addresses.

To make a domain the default

1. Sign in to the AWS Management Console and open the Amazon WorkMail console at https://console.aws. amazon.com/workmail/.

2. If necessary, change the region. From the navigation bar, select the region that meets your needs. For more information, see Regions and Endpoints in the *Amazon Web Services General Reference*.

3. On the **Organizations** screen, in the **Alias** column, select the name of the organization to which to add a default domain.

4. In the list of domains, select the check box next to the domain name and choose **Set as default**.

Verify Domains

To verify a domain with Amazon WorkMail, you initiate the process using the Amazon WorkMail console, and then publish a TXT record to your DNS server as described in Verifying Domains in Amazon SES in the *Amazon Simple Email Service Developer Guide*. This section contains the following topics that might help you if you encounter problems:

- To verify that the TXT record is correctly published to your DNS server, see How to Check Domain Verification Settings.
- For some common problems you may encounter when you attempt to verify your domain with Amazon WorkMail, see Common Domain Verification Problems.

How to Check Domain Verification Settings

You can check that your Amazon WorkMail domain verification TXT record is published correctly to your DNS server by using the following procedure. This procedure uses the nslookup tool, which is available for Windows and Linux. On Linux, you can also use dig.

The commands in these instructions were executed on Windows 7, and the example domain we use is *example.com*.

In this procedure, you first find the DNS servers that serve your domain, and then query those servers to view the TXT records. You query the DNS servers that serve your domain because those servers contain the most up-to-date information for your domain, which can take time to propagate to other DNS servers.

To verify that your domain verification TXT record is published to your DNS server

1. Find the name servers for your domain:

    1. Open a command prompt. To open a command prompt on Windows 7, choose **Start** and type **cmd**. On Linux-based operating systems, open a terminal window.

    2. At the command prompt, type the following, where is your domain. This lists all of the name servers that serve your domain.

       ```
       1. nslookup -type=NS <domain>
       ```

       If your domain was *example.com*, this command would look like:

       ```
       1. nslookup -type=NS example.com
       ```

       The command's output list the name servers that serve your domain. You query one of these servers in the next step.

2. Verify that the TXT record is correctly published:

    1. At the command prompt, type the following, where is your domain, and is one of the name servers you found in step 1.

       ```
       1. nslookup -type=TXT  _amazonses.<domain> <name server>
       ```

       In this *example.com* example, if the name server in step 1 was called *ns1.name-server.net*, you would type the following:

       ```
       1. nslookup -type=TXT  _amazonses.example.com ns1.name-server.net
       ```

    2. In the output of the command, verify that the string that follows `text =` matches the TXT value you see when you select the domain in the Verified Senders list of the Amazon WorkMail console.

       In the example, you are looking for a TXT record under *_amazonses.example.com* with a value of `fmxqxT/icOYx4aA/bEUrDPMeax9/s3frblS+niixmqk=`. If the record is correctly published, the command should have the following output:

       ```
       1. _amazonses.example.com text = "fmxqxT/icOYx4aA/bEUrDPMeax9/s3frblS+niixmqk="
       ```

To verify that your domain verification MX record is published to your DNS server

1. Find the name servers for your domain:

    1. Open a command prompt. To open a command prompt on Windows 7, choose **Start** and type **cmd**. On Linux-based operating systems, open a terminal window.

    2. At the command prompt, type the following, where is your domain. This lists all of the name servers that serve your domain.

       ```
       1. nslookup -type=NS <domain>
       ```

If your domain was *example.com*, this command would look like:

```
1 1. nslookup -type=NS example.com
```

The command's output lists the name servers that serve your domain. You query one of these servers in the next step.

2. Verify that the MX record is correctly published:

   1. At the command prompt, type the following, where is your domain, and is one of the name servers you found in step 1.

   ```
   1 1. nslookup -type=MX <domain> <name server>
   ```

   In the *example.com* example, if the name server in step 1 is called *ns1.name-server.net*, you would type the following:

   ```
   1 1. nslookup -type=MX example.com ns1.name-server.net
   ```

   2. In the output of the command, verify that the string that follows `mail exchange` `=` matches one of the following values:

   For the US East (N. Virginia) Region, the record must be: `10 inbound-smtp.us-east-1.amazonaws.com`

   For the EU (Ireland) Region, the record must be: `10 inbound-smtp.eu-west-1.amazonaws.com`

   For the US West (Oregon) Region, the record must be: `10 inbound-smtp.us-west-2.amazonaws.com` **Note**
   10 represents the MX preference number or priority.

Common Domain Verification Problems

If you have any issues with domain verification, see the list below for possible solutions.

- **Your DNS provider does not allow underscores in TXT record names** — You can omit _amazonses from the TXT record name.

- **You want to verify the same domain multiple times and you can't have multiple TXT records with the same name** — You might need to verify your domain more than one time because you're sending in different regions or you're sending from multiple AWS accounts from the same domain in the same region. If your DNS provider does not allow you to have multiple TXT records with the same name, there are two workarounds. The first workaround, if your DNS provider allows it, is to assign multiple values to the TXT record. For example, if your DNS is managed by Amazon Route 53, you can set up multiple values for the same TXT record as follows:

  1. In the Amazon Route 53 console, choose the _amazonses TXT record that you added when you verified your domain in the first region.

  2. For **Value**, press **Enter** after the first value.

  3. Add the value for the additional region, and save the record set.

  If you only need to verify your domain twice, another workaround you can try is to verify it one time with _amazonses in the TXT record name and then omit _amazonses from the record name entirely. We recommend the multiple value solution as a best practice.

- **Amazon WorkMail reports that domain verification failed**— The domain displays a status of "failed" in the **Domains** tab of the Amazon WorkMail console. This means that Amazon WorkMail cannot find the necessary TXT record on your DNS server. Verify that the required TXT record is correctly published to your DNS server by using the procedure in How to Check Domain Verification Settings, and look for the following possible error.

  - **Your DNS provider appended the domain name to the end of the TXT record**—Adding a TXT record that already contains the domain name (such as _amazonses.example.com) may result in the duplication of the domain name (such as _amazonses.example.com.example.com). To avoid duplication of the domain name, add a period to the end of the domain name in the TXT record. This indicates to your DNS provider that the record name is fully qualified (that is, no longer relative to the domain name), and prevents the DNS provider from appending an additional domain name.

Edit Domain Identity Policies

Domain identity policies specify permissions for email actions (such as redirecting emails). You can redirect email to any email address of your choosing; however, if your domain was added prior to October 13, 2016, you need to update the sending authorization policy manually to support that.

The update is the addition of a new action: `ses:*`. Domains added after October 13, 2016 have this added by default.

Note
Exercise caution when editing other sections of the `ses` policy, as incorrect settings can have an adverse effect on Amazon WorkMail functionality.

To update the domain identity policy

1. Sign in to the AWS Management Console and open the Amazon SES console at https://console.aws. amazon.com/ses/home.

2. In the **Navigation** pane of the Amazon SES console, under **Identity Management**, choose **Domains**.

3. In the list of domains, select the domain to edit.

4. In the **Details** pane, expand **Identity Policies**, find the policy to edit, and then choose **Edit Policy**.

5. In the **Edit Policy** pane, under "Action", add `ses:*`,.

6. Choose **Apply Policy**.

The updated actions of the policy should look like the following:

```
1    "Action": [
2        "ses:*",
3        "ses:SendBounce",
4        "ses:SendRawEmail"
5    ],
```

Authenticate Email with SPF

The Sender Policy Framework (SPF) is an email validation standard designed to combat email spoofing. For information about configuring SPF for your Amazon WorkMail-enabled domain, see Authenticating Email with SPF in Amazon SES.

Working with Resources

Amazon WorkMail can help your users reserve resources, such as meeting rooms or equipment (projectors, phones, cars, and so on). To book a resource, the user adds the resource to the meeting invite.

Topics

- Create a Resource
- Edit a Resource
- Remove a Resource

Create a Resource

You can add a new resource to your organization, and allow it to be reserved.

To add a resource

1. Open the Amazon WorkMail console at https://console.aws.amazon.com/workmail/.

2. If necessary, change the region. From the navigation bar, choose the region that meets your needs. For more information, see Regions and Endpoints in the *Amazon Web Services General Reference*.

3. On the **Organizations** page, select your organization.

4. In the navigation pane, choose **Resources** and **Add resource**.

5. On the **Add resource details** page, enter values for the **Resource name**, **Description**, **Resource type**, and **Email address** fields.

6. Choose **Create**.

Edit a Resource

You can edit a resource's general details (name, description, type, and email address), booking options, and delegates.

To edit general resource details

1. Open the Amazon WorkMail console at https://console.aws.amazon.com/workmail/.

2. If necessary, change the region. From the navigation bar, choose the region that meets your needs. For more information, see Regions and Endpoints in the *Amazon Web Services General Reference*.

3. On the **Organizations** page, select your organization.

4. In the navigation pane, choose **Resources**, and select the resource to edit.

5. On the **General** tab, update the details to change: **Resource name**, **Description**, **Resource Type**, or **Email address**.

6. Choose **Save**.

You can configure a resource to accept or decline booking requests automatically.

To enable or disable automatic processing of booking requests

1. Open the Amazon WorkMail console at https://console.aws.amazon.com/workmail/.

2. If necessary, change the region. From the navigation bar, choose the region that meets your needs. For more information, see Regions and Endpoints in the *Amazon Web Services General Reference*.

3. On the **Organizations** page, select your organization.

4. In the navigation pane, choose **Resources**, and then select the resource to edit.

5. On the **Booking Options** tab, choose **Edit**.

6. To accept all resource requests automatically, select **Automatically accept all resource requests**.

7. To decline recurring resource requests automatically, select **Automatically decline recurring resource requests**.

8. To decline conflicting resource requests automatically, select **Automatically decline conflicting resource requests**.

9. Choose **Save**.

You can add a delegate to control booking requests for a resource. Resource delegates automatically receive copies of all booking requests and have full access to the resource calendar. In addition, they must accept all booking requests for a resource.

To add a resource delegate Note
Before you proceed, follow the process above to clear the **Automatically accept all resource requests** option.

1. Open the Amazon WorkMail console at https://console.aws.amazon.com/workmail/.

2. If necessary, change the region. From the navigation bar, choose the region that meets your needs. For more information, see Regions and Endpoints in the *Amazon Web Services General Reference*.

3. On the **Organizations** page, select your organization.

4. In the navigation pane, choose **Resources**, and select the name of the resource to edit.

5. On the **Delegates** tab, choose **Edit**.

6. Select the users or groups to add as delegates, and then use the right arrow to add them to the delegate list.

7. Choose **Save**.

Remove a Resource

When you no longer need a resource, you can remove it.

To remove a resource

1. Open the Amazon WorkMail console at https://console.aws.amazon.com/workmail/.

2. If necessary, change the region. From the navigation bar, choose the region that meets your needs. For more information, see Regions and Endpoints in the *Amazon Web Services General Reference.*

3. On the **Organizations** page, select the organization.

4. In the navigation pane, choose **Resources**.

5. In the list of resources, select the resource to remove, and choose **Remove**.

6. In the **Remove resource(s)** dialog box, choose **Remove**.

Migrating to Amazon WorkMail

You can migrate to Amazon WorkMail from Microsoft Exchange, Microsoft Office 365, G Suite Basic (formerly Google Apps for Work), and many other platforms by working with one of our partners. For more information about our partners, see Migrate to Amazon WorkMail for Free.

Topics

- Step 1: Create or Enable Users in Amazon WorkMail
- Step 2: Migrate to Amazon WorkMail
- Step 3: Complete the Migration to Amazon WorkMail

Step 1: Create or Enable Users in Amazon WorkMail

Before you can migrate your users, you must add the users in Amazon WorkMail to provision the mailbox. For more information, see Create New Users.

Step 2: Migrate to Amazon WorkMail

You can work with any of our migration partners to migrate to Amazon WorkMail. For information about about these providers, see Amazon WorkMail.

In order to migrate your mailboxes, you can assign an Amazon WorkMail user as the migration administrator. You can specify the migration administrator in the following ways:

- Add the new user **migration_admin** in the Amazon WorkMail console or create the user **migration_admin** in your Active Directory and enable this user for Amazon WorkMail.
- In the Amazon WorkMail console, on the **Organizations settings** screen, under **Migration settings**, choose **Edit**, and then specify a user that you've designated as the migration administrator for the **migration_admin** field.

Step 3: Complete the Migration to Amazon WorkMail

After you have migrated your email accounts to Amazon WorkMail, you need to verify your DNS records and configure your desktop and mobile clients.

To complete migration to Amazon WorkMail

1. Verify that all DNS records are updated and that they point to Amazon WorkMail. For more information about the required DNS records, see Add a Domain. **Note**
The DNS record update process may take several hours. If any new items appear in a source mailbox while the MX records are being changed, you can re-run the migration tool to migrate new items after the DNS records are updated.

2. Configure your desktop and mobile clients to use Amazon WorkMail. For more information about configuring your desktop or mobile clients, see Connect Microsoft Outlook to Your Amazon WorkMail Account in the *Amazon WorkMail User Guide*.

Interoperability Between Amazon WorkMail and Microsoft Exchange

Interoperability allows you to minimize disruption to your users as you migrate mailboxes to Amazon WorkMail, or use Amazon WorkMail for a subset of your corporate mailboxes.

Interoperability between Amazon WorkMail and Microsoft Exchange Server allows you to use the same corporate domain for mailboxes across both environments so that your users can seamlessly schedule meetings with bi-directional sharing of calendar free/busy information.

Prerequisites

Before you enable interoperability with Microsoft Exchange, complete the following tasks.

- To configure the availability settings for Microsoft Exchange, you need to have at least one user enabled for Amazon WorkMail. To enable a user, follow the steps in Enable Email Routing for a User.
- Set up an Active Directory (AD) Connector—Setting up an AD Connector with your on-premises directory allows users to continue using their existing corporate credentials. For more information, Set up AD Connector and Integrate Amazon WorkMail with your on-premises directory.
- Set up your Amazon WorkMail organization—Create an Amazon WorkMail organization that uses the AD Connector referenced above.
- Add domains to your Amazon WorkMail organization—Add your corporate domains to Amazon WorkMail. Ensure that your domain has been verified in the Amazon WorkMail console; otherwise, emails sent to this alias will bounce. For more information, see Working with Domains.
- Migrate mailboxes—Enable users to provision and migrate mailboxes from your on-premises environment to Amazon WorkMail. For more information, see Enable Existing Users and see Migrating to Amazon WorkMail. **Note**
  DNS records must not be updated to point to Amazon WorkMail. This ensures that Microsoft Exchange remains the primary server for incoming email for as long as you would like to have interoperability between the two environments.
- Make sure that the User Principal Names (UPNs) in Active Directory match the users' primary SMTP addresses.

Amazon WorkMail makes HTTPS requests to the EWS URL on Microsoft Exchange to obtain calendar free/busy information.

- Ensure that the relevant firewall settings are set up to allow access from the Internet. The default port for HTTPS requests is port 443.
- Amazon WorkMail can only make successful HTTPS requests to the EWS URL on Microsoft Exchange when a certificate signed by a valid certificate authority (CA) is available on your Microsoft Exchange environment. For more information, see V-Exchange on Microsoft TechNet. For more information about importing a certificate, see Importing Certificates on Microsoft TechNet.
- You need to enable **Basic Authentication** for EWS on your Microsoft Exchange. For more information, see [Virtual Directories: Exchange 2013](https://blogs.msdn.microsoft.com/mvpawardprogram/2013/03/18/virtual-directories- exchange-2013/) on the Microsoft MVP Award Program Blog.

Add Domains and Enable Mailboxes

Add your corporate domains to Amazon WorkMail so that they can be used in email addresses. Ensure that the domains added to Amazon WorkMail are verified, then enable users and groups to provision mailboxes on Amazon WorkMail. Resources cannot be enabled in Amazon WorkMail while in interoperability mode, and should be re-created in Amazon WorkMail after you disable interoperability mode. However, you can still use them to schedule meetings while in interoperability mode. Resources from Microsoft Exchange are always shown in the **Users** tab in Amazon WorkMail.

- For more information, see Add Domains, Enable Existing Users, and Enable an Existing Group.

Note

To ensure interoperability with Microsoft Exchange, do not update the DNS records to point to Amazon WorkMail records. Microsoft Exchange remains the primary server for incoming email as long as you would like to have interoperability between the two environments.

Enable Interoperability

If you have not created an Amazon WorkMail organization, follow the steps in Integrate Amazon WorkMail with your on-premises directory (Custom Setup) and choose **Enable interoperability** when creating your Amazon WorkMail organization.

If you already have an Amazon WorkMail organization with an AD Connector linked to your Microsoft Active Directory and you also have Microsoft Exchange, contact AWS Support for assistance with enabling Microsoft Exchange interoperability for an existing Amazon WorkMail organization.

Create Service Accounts in Microsoft Exchange and Amazon WorkMail

To access calendar free/busy information, you need to create a service account on both Microsoft Exchange and Amazon WorkMail. The Microsoft Exchange service account is any user on Microsoft Exchange that has access to the calendar free/busy information of other users on the environment. Access is granted by default; no special permissions are needed.

Similarly, the Amazon WorkMail service account is any user on Amazon WorkMail that has access to calendar free/busy information of other users on Amazon WorkMail (which is granted by default).

Using an Amazon WorkMail organization that leverages an AD Connector integrated with your on-premises directory means that the Amazon WorkMail service account user must be created in your on-premises directory and then enabled for Amazon WorkMail.

Limitations in Interoperability Mode

When your organization is in interoperability mode, all user, group, and resource management must be done using the Exchange Admin Center. Users and groups can be enabled for Amazon WorkMail through the AWS Management Console. For more information, see Enable Existing Users and Enable an Existing Group.

When enabling a user or group for Amazon WorkMail, you cannot edit the email addresses or aliases of those users and groups. Those must also be configured via the Exchange Admin Center. Amazon WorkMail synchronizes changes in your directory every four hours.

Resources cannot be created or enabled in Amazon WorkMail while in interoperability mode. However, all your Exchange resources are available in the Amazon WorkMail address book and can be used for scheduling meetings as usual.

Enable Email Routing Between Microsoft Exchange and Amazon WorkMail Users

When you enable email routing between Microsoft Exchange Server and Amazon WorkMail, users that are configured for Amazon WorkMail can continue using their existing email addresses to send and receive email on Amazon WorkMail. When email routing is enabled, your Microsoft Exchange Server remains the primary SMTP server for incoming email.

Prerequisites for email routing:

- Interoperability mode is enabled for your organization. For more information, see Enable Interoperability.
- Your domain is added and verified in the Amazon WorkMail console.
- Your Microsoft Exchange Server can send email to the Internet. You may need to configure a Send connector. For more information, see Create a Send connector for email sent to the Internet on Microsoft TechNet.

Enable Email Routing for a User

We recommend that you carry out the following steps first for test users, before applying the change to your organization.

1. Enable the user you are migrating to Amazon WorkMail. For more information, see Enable Existing Users.

2. In the Amazon WorkMail console, ensure that there are at least two email addresses associated with the enabled user.

   - **workmailuser@orgname.awsapps.com** (this is added automatically, and can be used for tests without your Microsoft Exchange.)

   - **workmailuser@yourdomain.com** (this is added automatically, and is the primary Microsoft Exchange address.)

     For more information, see Edit User Email Addresses.

3. Ensure that you migrate all data from the mailbox in Microsoft Exchange to the mailbox in Amazon WorkMail. For more information, see Migrating to Amazon WorkMail.

4. When all the data is migrated, disable the mailbox for the user on Microsoft Exchange and create a mail user (or mail-enabled user) that has the external SMTP address pointed to Amazon WorkMail. This can be achieved using the following commands in Exchange Management Shell. **Important**
   The steps below erase the contents of the mailbox. Ensure that your data has been migrated to Amazon WorkMail before you attempt to enable email routing. Some mail clients do not seamlessly switch to Amazon WorkMail when this command is executed. For more information, see Mail Client Configuration.

```
1 $old_mailbox = Get-Mailbox exchangeuser
```

```
1 Disable-Mailbox $old_mailbox
```

```
1 $new_mailuser = Enable-MailUser $old_mailbox.Identity -ExternalEmailAddress
     workmailuser@orgname.awsapps.com -PrimarySmtpAddress $old_mailbox.PrimarySmtpAddress
```

```
1 Set-MailUser $new_mailuser -EmailAddresses $old_mailbox.EmailAddresses -
     HiddenFromAddressListsEnabled $old_mailbox.HiddenFromAddressListsEnabled
```

In the above commands, **orgname** represents the name of the Amazon WorkMail organization. For more information, see Disabling Mailbox and Enabling Mail Users on Microsoft TechNet.

5. Send a test email to the user (as per the example above, **workmailuser@yourdomain.com**). If email routing has been enabled correctly, the user should be able to log in to the Amazon WorkMail mailbox and receive the email.

Note

Microsoft Exchange remains the primary server for incoming email as long as you would like to have interoperability between the two environments. To ensure interoperability with Microsoft Exchange, the DNS records should not be updated to point to Amazon WorkMail until later.

Post Setup Configuration

The above steps moves a user mailbox from Microsoft Exchange Server to Amazon WorkMail, while keeping the user in Microsoft Exchange as a contact. Because the migrated user is now an external mail user, Microsoft Exchange Server imposes additional constraints and there may be additional configuration requirements to complete the migration.

- The user might not be able to send emails to groups by default. To enable this functionality, the user needs to be added to a safe sender list for all groups. For more information, see Delivery management on Microsoft TechNet.
- The user also might not be able to book resources. To enable this functionality, you need to set the `ProcessExternalMeetingMessages` of all resources that the user needs to access. For more information, see Set-CalendarProcessing on Microsoft TechNet.

Mail Client Configuration

Some mail clients do not switch seamlessly to Amazon WorkMail and require the user to perform additional setup. Different mail clients require different actions to be taken.

- Microsoft Outlook on Windows—Requires MS Outlook to be restarted. At startup, you are required to choose whether to keep using the old mailbox or use a temporary mailbox. Choose the temporary mailbox option, and reconfigure the Microsoft Exchange mailbox from scratch.
- Microsoft Outlook on MacOS—When Outlook is restarted, you see the following message **Outlook was redirected to server orgname.awsapps.com. Do you want this server to configure your settings?**. Accept the suggestion.
- Mail on iOS—The mail app stops receiving emails and generates a **Cannot get mail** error. Reconfigure the Microsoft Exchange mailbox from scratch.

Configure Availability Settings on Amazon WorkMail

Configure availability settings on Amazon WorkMail and Microsoft Exchange to enable bi-directional sharing of calendar free/busy information.

To configure availability settings in the console

1. Open the Amazon WorkMail console at https://console.aws.amazon.com/workmail/.

2. In the navigation panel, choose **Organization settings**, **Interoperability Settings**.

3. Choose **Configure availability settings** and provide the following information:

- **Domain**—The domain for which to set interoperability between Amazon WorkMail and Microsoft Exchange.
- **Exchange Web Services (EWS) URL**—The URL to which Amazon WorkMail sends HTTPS requests to access calendar free/busy information of users on Microsoft Exchange. The EWS URL usually looks like the following: **https://servername.com/EWS/Exchange.asmx**. You can obtain the EWS URL in one of the following ways: +

Using Microsoft Outlook

```
1 1. Log in to Microsoft Outlook on Windows for any user on your Exchange environment\.
2
3 1. Hold the **Ctrl** key and open the context \(right\-click\) menu on the Microsoft Outlook
     icon in the task bar\.
4
5 1. Choose **Test E\-mail AutoConfiguration**\.
6
7 1. Enter the Microsoft Exchange 'users email address and password, and choose **Test**\.
8
9 1. From the Results window, copy the value for the **Availability Service URL**\.
```

-

Using PowerShell +

```
1   ```
2   Get-WebServicesVirtualDirectory |Select name, *url* | fl
3   ```
4
5 The external URL returned by the above command is the EWS URL\.
```

- **User email address and password**—These are the credentials of the Microsoft Exchange service account and are encrypted and securely stored by Amazon WorkMail. The email address of the Microsoft Exchange service account should use the Fully Qualified Domain Name (FQDN). For more information, see Create Service Accounts in Microsoft Exchange and Amazon WorkMail.

  If your Active Directory domain is not the same as your Microsoft Exchange domain, use the User Principal Name (UPN) of the Microsoft Exchange Service account. This can be obtained with the following PowerShell command:

  ```
  1 Get-ADUser exchange_service_account_username | select UserPrincipalName
  ```

  In the above example, **exchange_service_account_username** is the username of the Microsoft Exchange Service account.

Configure Availability Settings in Microsoft Exchange

To redirect all calendar free/busy information requests for enabled users to Amazon WorkMail, set up an availability address space on Microsoft Exchange.

Use the following PowerShell command:

```
1  $credentials = Get-Credential
```

At the prompt, enter the credentials of the Amazon WorkMail service account. The username should be entered as **domain\username** (i.e., **orgname.awsapps.com\workmail_service_account_username**. Here, **orgname** represents the name of the Amazon WorkMail organization. For more information, see Create Service Accounts in Microsoft Exchange and Amazon WorkMail.

```
1  Add-AvailabilityAddressSpace -ForestName orgname.awsapps.com -AccessMethod OrgWideFB -
      Credentials $credentials
```

For more information, see Add-AvailabilityAddressSpace on Microsoft TechNet.

Disabling Interoperability and Decommissioning Your Mail Server

After all your Microsoft Exchange mailboxes are configured for Amazon WorkMail, you can disable interoperability. If you have not migrated any users or records, disabling interoperability does not affect any of your configurations.

Warning

Before disabling interoperability, ensure that you have completed all the required steps. Failure to do so could result in bounced emails or unintended behavior. If you have not completed migration, disabling interoperability may cause disruptions to your organization. You cannot undo this operation.

To disable interoperability support

1. Open the Amazon WorkMail console at https://console.aws.amazon.com/workmail/.

2. If necessary, change the region. From the navigation bar, choose the region that meets your needs. For more information, see Regions and Endpoints in the *Amazon Web Services General Reference*.

3. On the **Organizations** page, choose the organization that has interoperability mode enabled and choose **Disable Interoperability**.

4. In the **Disable interoperability with Microsoft Exchange** dialog box, enter the name of the organization and choose **Disable**.

After disabling interoperability support, users and groups that are not enabled for Amazon WorkMail are removed from the address book. You can still enable any missing user or group using the Amazon WorkMail console and they are added to the address book. Resources from Microsoft Exchange cannot be enabled and do not appear in the address book until you complete the step below.

- **Create resources in Amazon WorkMail**—You can create resources in Amazon WorkMail and configure delegates and booking options for these resources. For more information, see Working with Resources.
- **Create an AutoDiscover DNS record**—Configure an AutoDiscover DNS record for all mail domains in the organization to enable users to easily connect to their Amazon WorkMail mailboxes from their Microsoft Outlook and mobile clients. For more information, see Use AutoDiscover to Configure Endpoints.
- **Switch your MX DNS record to Amazon WorkMail**—To deliver all incoming emails to Amazon WorkMail, you have to switch your MX DNS record to Amazon WorkMail. It can take up to 72 hours before the DNS change is propagated to all DNS servers.
- **Decommission your mail server**—After you've verified that all email is being routed directly to Amazon WorkMail, you can decommission your mail server if you do not intend to use it going forward.

Troubleshooting

Solutions to the most commonly encountered Amazon WorkMail interoperability and migration errors are listed below.

Exchange Web Services (EWS) URL is invalid or unreachable—Check that you have the correct EWS URL. For more information, see Configure Availability Settings on Amazon WorkMail.

Connection failure during EWS validation—This is a general error, and can be caused by:

- No Internet connection in Microsoft Exchange.
- Your firewall is not configured to allow access from the Internet. Ensure that port 443 (the default port for HTTPS requests) is open.

If you've confirmed the Internet connection and firewall settings, but the error persists, contact AWS Support.

Invalid username and password when configuring Microsoft Exchange interoperability.—This is a general error, and can be caused by:

- The username is not in the expected form. Use the following pattern:

1 `DOMAIN\username`

- Your Microsoft Exchange server is not configured for Basic Authentication for EWS. For more information, see [Virtual Directories: Exchange 2013](https://blogs.msdn.microsoft.com/mvpawardprogram/2013/03/18/virtual-directories- exchange-2013/) on the Microsoft MVP Award Program Blog.

User receives emails with winmail.dat attachment—This might happen when encrypted S/MIME email is sent from Exchange to Amazon WorkMail and received in Outlook for Mac 2016 or IMAP client. The solution is to run the following command in Exchange Management Shell:

Set-RemoteDomain -Identity "Default" -TNEFEnabled $false

If you've confirmed the points above but the error persists, contact AWS Support.

Using Email Journaling with Amazon WorkMail

You can set up journaling to record your email communication, using integrated third-party archiving and eDiscovery tools. This ensures that email storage compliance regulations for privacy protection, data storage, and information protection are met.

Using Journaling

Amazon WorkMail journals all emails that are sent to any user in the specified organization, as well as all emails sent by users in that organization. A copy of all emails is sent to an address specified by the system administrator, in a format called `journal record`. This format is compatible with Microsoft email programs. There is no additional charge for email journaling.

Two email addresses are used for email journaling—a journaling email address and a report email address. The journaling email address is the address of a dedicated mailbox or third-party device that is integrated with your account, where journal reports are sent. The report email address is the address of your system administrator, where notifications of failed journal reports are sent.

All journal records are sent from an email address that is automatically added to your domain and looks like the following:

```
1 amazonjournaling@yourorganization.awsapps.com
```

There is no mailbox associated with this address, and you will not be able to create one using this name or address.

Note
Do not delete the following domain record from the Amazon SES console, or email journaling stops functioning:

```
1 yourorganization.awsapps.com
```

Every incoming or outgoing email generates one journal record, regardless of the number of recipients or user groups. Email that fails to generate a journal record generates an error notification, which is sent to the report email address.

To enable email journaling

1. Open the Amazon WorkMail console at https://console.aws.amazon.com/workmail/.

2. On the **Organization settings** screen, choose **Journaling Settings**, **Edit**, **On**.

3. For **Journaling email address**, enter the email address provided by your email journaling provider.
   Note
   We recommend using a dedicated journaling provider.

4. For **Report email address**, enter the email administrator's address.

5. Choose **Save**. The changes are applied immediately.

Managing Email Flows

You can set up *email flow rules* for handling incoming email based on a sender's email address or domain. These flow rules help prevent email from undesirable senders reaching your users' mailboxes. Unlike email rules for individual mailboxes, email flow rules automatically apply to all email sent to anyone inside the Amazon WorkMail organization.

To create an email flow rule, you specify a *rule action* to apply to an email when a specified *sender pattern* is matched.

Topics

- Rule Actions
- Sender Patterns
- Creating an Email Flow Rule
- Testing an Email Flow Rule
- Modifying an Email Flow Rule
- Removing an Email Flow Rule

Rule Actions

Email flow rules define how incoming email is handled. For each rule, you specify sender patterns together with one of the following actions.

Action	Description
Drop	The email is ignored. It is not delivered, and the sender is not notified of the non-delivery.
Bounce	The email is not delivered, and the sender is notified of the non-delivery using a bounce message.
Deliver to junk folder	The email is delivered to users' spam folders, even if it is not originally detected to be spam by the Amazon WorkMail spam detection system.
Default	The email is delivered according to detection by the Amazon WorkMail spam detection system. If it is detected as spam, it's delivered to the junk folder. Otherwise, it's delivered to the inbox. All other less specific email flow rules are ignored. This action can be used to add exceptions to domain-based rules by configuring it with a more specific sender pattern. For more information, see Sender Patterns.
Never deliver to junk folder	The email is always delivered to users' inboxes, even if it is marked as spam by the Amazon WorkMail spam detection system. Bypassing the default spam detection system could expose your users to high-risk content from the addresses that you specify.

Note

Incoming mail is first delivered to Amazon SES and then to Amazon WorkMail. If an incoming email is dropped by Amazon SES (for example, when a known virus is detected or because of explicit IP filtering rules), specifying a delivery action (for example, **Default**, **Deliver to junk folder**, or **Never deliver to junk folder**) has no effect.

Sender Patterns

An email flow rule can apply to a specific email address, or all email addresses under a specific domain or set of domains. You define a sender pattern to determine the email addresses to which a rule applies.

A sender pattern can take one of the following forms:

- **An email address** matches a single email address; for example:

1 `mailbox@domain.com`

- **A domain name** matches all email addresses under that domain; for example:

1 `domain.com`

- **A wildcard domain** matches all email addresses under that domain and all of its subdomains. A wildcard can only appear at the front of a domain; for example:

1 `*.domain.com`

- **Star** matches any email addresses under any domain.

1 `*`

Multiple patterns can be specified for one rule. For more information, see Rule Actions. If either the `Sender` or `From` header in an incoming email matches any patterns, an email flow rule is applied. If present, the `Sender` address is matched first. The `From` address is matched if there is no `Sender` header or if the `Sender` header doesn't match any rule.

If multiple rules match, the action of the most specific rule is applied; for example, a rule for a specific email address takes precedence over a rule for an entire domain. If multiple rules have the same specificity, the most restrictive action is applied; for example, a **Drop** action takes precedence over a **Bounce** action. The order of precedence for actions is the same as the order in which they are listed in Rule Actions.

Note
Take care when creating rules with overlapping sender patterns with **Drop** or **Bounce** actions. Unexpected precedence ordering could result in chunks of incoming email not being delivered.

Creating an Email Flow Rule

To create an email flow rule, you specify a rule action to apply to an email when a specified sender pattern is matched. When you create a new email flow rule, it's applied immediately.

To create a new email flow rule

1. Open the Amazon WorkMail console at https://console.aws.amazon.com/workmail/.

2. In the navigation pane, choose **Organization settings, Email flow rules**.

3. Choose **Create Rule**.

4. Enter a name for your rule and one or more sender patterns.

5. Select the action to apply to the email.

6. Choose **Create Rule**.

If you want, you can test the new email flow rule that you created. For more information, see Testing an Email Flow Rule.

Testing an Email Flow Rule

To check your current rule configuration, you can test how the configuration will behave against specific email addresses.

To test an email flow rule

1. Open the Amazon WorkMail console at https://console.aws.amazon.com/workmail/.

2. In the navigation pane, choose **Organization settings**, **Email flow rules**.

3. Next to **Test configuration**, enter a full email address to test.

4. Choose **Test**. The action that will be taken for the provided email address is displayed

Modifying an Email Flow Rule

You can modify the rule action or sender pattern for an email flow rule. When you modify an email flow rule, the changes are applied immediately.

To modify email flow rule

1. Open the Amazon WorkMail console at https://console.aws.amazon.com/workmail/.

2. In the navigation pane, choose **Organization settings**, **Email flow rules**.

3. Select the rule and choose **Edit**.

4. Change the sender patterns or action as required.

5. Choose **Save**.

If you want, you can test the new email flow rule that you created. For more information, see Testing an Email Flow Rule.

Removing an Email Flow Rule

When you remove an email flow rule, the changes are applied immediately.

To remove an email flow rule

1. Open the Amazon WorkMail console at https://console.aws.amazon.com/workmail/.

2. In the navigation pane, choose **Organization settings**, **Email flow rules**.

3. Select the rule and choose **Remove**.

4. In the confirmation dialog, choose **Remove**.

Best Practices

Take advantage of these best practices to maximize your experience with Amazon WorkMail.

Topics

- Use AutoDiscover to Configure Endpoints

Use AutoDiscover to Configure Endpoints

AutoDiscover enables you to easily configure Microsoft Outlook and mobile clients with only your email address and password. The service also maintains a connection to Amazon WorkMail and updates local settings whenever endpoint or settings changes are made. In addition, AutoDiscover enables your client to use additional Amazon WorkMail features, such as the Offline Address Book, Out-of-Office Assistant, and the ability to view free/busy time in Calendar.

The client performs the following AutoDiscover phases to detect the server endpoint URLs:

- Phase 1: The client performs an SCP lookup against the local Active Directory. If your client isn't domain-joined, AutoDiscover skips this step.
- Phase 2: The client sends a request to the following URLs and validates the results. These endpoints are only available using HTTPS.
  - https://company/.tld/autodiscover/autodiscover/.xml
  - https://autodiscover/.company/.tld/autodiscover/autodiscover/.xml
- Phase 3: The client performs a DNS lookup to autodiscover.company.tld and sends an unauthenticated GET request to the derived endpoint from the user's email address. If the server returns a 302 redirect, the client resends the AutoDiscover request against the returned HTTPS endpoint.

If all of these phases fail, the client can't be configured automatically, and you must set up the client manually. For information about manually configuring mobile devices, see Manually Connect Your Device.

When you set up your domain in Amazon WorkMail, you are prompted to add the AutoDiscover DNS record. This enables the client to perform phase 3 of the AutoDiscover process. However, these steps don't work for all mobile devices, such as the stock Android email app, and you may need to set up AutoDiscover phase 2 manually.

There are two ways you can set up AutoDiscover phase 2 for your domain:

- By using Route 53 and Amazon CloudFront (recommended)
- By setting up an Apache web server with a reverse proxy

To enable AutoDiscover phase 2 with Route 53 and CloudFront Note
The following steps show how to proxy https://autodiscover/.company/.tld/autodiscover/autodiscover/.xml/. To proxy https://company/.tld/autodiscover/autodiscover/.xml, remove the "autodiscover." prefix from the domains in the following steps.
For more information about applicable pricing, see Amazon CloudFront Pricing and Amazon Route 53 Pricing.

1. Get an SSL certificate for autodiscover.company.tld and upload it to IAM. For more information, see Working with Server Certificates.

2. Create a new CloudFront distribution.

    1. Open the CloudFront console at https://console.aws.amazon.com/cloudfront/.

    2. Choose **Create Distribution**, **Web** and **Get Started**.

    3. Fill in the following values for **Origin Settings**:

        - **Origin Domain Name:** autodiscover-service.mail.us-east-1.awsapps.com, autodiscover-service.mail.eu-west-1.awsapps.com, or autodiscover-service.mail.us-west-2.awsapps.com
        - **Origin Protocol Policy:** Match Viewer **Note**
        Leave **Origin path** blank, and do not change the auto-populated value for **Origin ID**.

    4. Fill in the following values for **Default Cache Behavior Settings**:

        - **Viewer Protocol Policy:** HTTPS Only
        - **Allowed HTTP Methods:** GET, HEAD, OPTIONS, PUT, POST, PATCH, DELETE
        - **Cache Based on Selected Request Headers:** All
        - **Forward Cookies:** All

- **Query String Forwarding and Caching**: None (Improves Caching)
- **Smooth Streaming**: No
- **Restrict Viewer Access**: No

5. Fill in the following values for **Distribution Settings**:

- **Price Class**: Use only US, Canada, and Europe
- **Alternate Domain Names (CNAMEs)**: autodiscover.company.tld (or company.tld)
- **SSL Certificate**: Custom SSL Certificate (stored in IAM)
- **Custom SSL Client Support**: All Clients **Note**
  Leave **Default Root Object** blank.
- **Logging**: Choose **On** or **Off**
- **Comment**: AutoDiscover type2 for autodiscover.company.tld
- For **Distribution State**, choose **Enabled**

3. In Route 53, connect the CloudFront distribution to DNS: **Note**
   These steps assume that the DNS record for company.tld is hosted in Route 53.

   1. In the Route 53 console, choose **Hosted Zones** and **company.tld**.

   2. Choose **Create Record Set**, and then fill in the following fields:

   - **Name**: autodiscover.company.tld
   - **Type**: A - IPv4 address
   - **Alias**: Yes
   - **Alias Target**: The CloudFront distribution created above **Note**
     If the CloudFront distribution created above is not present, wait a while and try again later.
     Change propagation for new CloudFront endpoints in Route 53 might take up to 1 hour.
   - **Evaluate Target Health**: No

   3. Choose **Create**.

To enable AutoDiscover phase 2 with an Apache web server

1. Configure the following two directives on an SSL-enabled Apache server:

```
1 SSLProxyEngine on ProxyPass /autodiscover/autodiscover.xml
2 https://autodiscover-service.mail.REGION.awsapps.com/autodiscover/autodiscover.xml
```

2. If they are not already enabled, enable the following Apache modules:

- proxy
- proxy_http
- socache_shmcb
- ssl

3. Confirm that the endpoint is SSL-enabled and configured correctly.

AutoDiscover Phase 2 Troubleshooting

To make a basic unauthorized request, create an unauthenticated POST request to the AutoDiscover endpoint and see if it returns a "401 unauthorized" message:

```
1 $ curl -X POST -v https://autodiscover.''company.tld''/autodiscover/autodiscover.xml
2 ...
3 HTTP/1.1 401 Unauthorized
```

If the basic request is unsuccessful and returns a "401 unauthorized" message, run a real request that a mobile device would issue.

To do this, first create a request.xml file with the following XML content:

```
1  <?xml version="1.0" encoding="utf-8"?>
2  <Autodiscover xmlns="http://schemas.microsoft.com/exchange/autodiscover/mobilesync/requestschema
       /2006">
3      <Request>
4              <EMailAddress>testuser@company.tld</EMailAddress>
5              <AcceptableResponseSchema>
6               http://schemas.microsoft.com/exchange/autodiscover/mobilesync/responseschema/2006
7              </AcceptableResponseSchema>
8      </Request>
9  </Autodiscover>
```

Second, make the request.

```
1  $ curl -d @request.xml -u testuser@company.tld -v https://autodiscover.company.tld/autodiscover/
       autodiscover.xml
2  Enter host password for user 'testuser@company.tld':
3  <?xml version="1.0" encoding="UTF-8"?>
4  <Autodiscover xmlns="http://schemas.microsoft.com/exchange/autodiscover/responseschema/2006"
       xmlns:xsd="http://www.w3.org/2001/XMLSchema" xmlns:xsi="http://www.w3.org/2001/XMLSchema-
       instance">
5  <Response xmlns="http://schemas.microsoft.com/exchange/autodiscover/mobilesync/responseschema
       /2006">
6      <Culture>en:us</Culture>
7      <User>
8          <DisplayName>User1</DisplayName>
9          <EMailAddress>testuser@company.tld</EMailAddress>
10     </User>
11     <Action>
12         <Settings>
13             <Server>
14                 <Type>MobileSync</Type>
15                 <Url>https://mobile.mail.us-east-1.awsapps.com/Microsoft-Server-ActiveSync</Url>
16                 <Name>https://mobile.mail.us-east-1.awsapps.com/Microsoft-Server-ActiveSync</
                       Name>
17             </Server>
18         </Settings>
19     </Action>
20 </Response>
```

If the response output is similar, your AutoDiscover endpoint is configured correctly.

Unsupported Attachment Types

You can send messages with attachments through Amazon WorkMail by using the Multipurpose Internet Mail Extensions (MIME) standard. Amazon WorkMail accepts all file attachment types except for attachments with the file extensions in the following list.

Note

Some ISPs have further limitations (such as archived attachments), so we recommend sending a test email through major ISPs before you send your production email.

The following attachment types aren't supported:

Unsupported Attachment Types

.ade .adp .app	.fxp	.gad-	.mag	.mam	.msc	.msh	.prg .reg .scf	.url .vb .vbe
.asp .bas .bat	get .hlp .hta		.maq	.mar	.msh1	.msh2	.scr .sct .shb	.vbs .vps .vs-
.cer .chm .cmd	.inf .ins .isp		.mas	.mat	.mshxml		.shs .sys .ps1	macros .vss
.com .cpl .crt	.its .js .jse .ksh		.mau	.mav	.msh1xml		.ps1xml .ps2	.vst .vsw .vxd
.csh .der .exe	.lib .lnk .mad		.maw		.msh2xml .msi		.ps2xml .psc1	.ws .wsc .wsf
	.maf		.mda	.mdb	.msp .mst .ops		.psc2 .tmp	.wsh .xnk
			.mde	.mdt	.pcd .pif .plg			
			.mdw	.mdz	.prf			

Logging Amazon WorkMail API Calls with AWS CloudTrail

Amazon WorkMail is integrated with AWS CloudTrail, a service that provides a record of actions taken by a user, role, or an AWS service. If you create a trail, you can enable continuous delivery of CloudTrail events to an Amazon S3 bucket, Amazon CloudWatch Logs, and Amazon CloudWatch Events. Using the information collected by CloudTrail, you can determine the request that was made to Amazon WorkMail, the IP address from which the request was made, who made the request, when it was made, and additional details.

For more information about CloudTrail, including how to configure and enable it, see the AWS CloudTrail User Guide.

Amazon WorkMail Information in CloudTrail

All Amazon WorkMail actions are logged by CloudTrail and are documented in the Amazon WorkMail API Reference. For example, calls to the `ListUsers`, `RegisterToWorkMail` and `DescribeGroup` APIs generate entries in the CloudTrail log files.

Every event or log entry contains information about who generated the request. The identity information helps you determine the following:

- Whether the request was made with root or IAM user credentials
- Whether the request was made with temporary security credentials for a role or federated user
- Whether the request was made by another AWS service

For more information, see the CloudTrail userIdentity Element.

You can also create a trail and store your log files in your Amazon S3 bucket for as long as needed, and define Amazon S3 lifecycle rules to archive or delete log files automatically. By default, your log files are encrypted with Amazon S3 server-side encryption (SSE).

To be notified of log file delivery, configure CloudTrail to publish Amazon SNS notifications when new log files are delivered. For more information, see Configuring Amazon SNS Notifications for CloudTrail.

You can also aggregate Amazon WorkMail log files from multiple AWS Regions and multiple AWS accounts into a single Amazon S3 bucket.

For more information, see Receiving CloudTrail Log Files from Multiple Regions and Receiving CloudTrail Log Files from Multiple Accounts.

Understanding Amazon WorkMail Log File Entries

A trail is a configuration that enables delivery of events as log files to an Amazon S3 bucket that you specify. CloudTrail log files contain one or more log entries. An event represents a single request from any source and includes information about the requested action, the date and time of the action, request parameters, and so on. CloudTrail log files are not an ordered stack trace of the public API calls, so they do not appear in any specific order.

The following example shows a CloudTrail log entry that demonstrates the `CreateUser` action.

```
1  {
2    "eventVersion": "1.05",
3    "userIdentity": {
4      "type": "IAMUser",
5      "principalId": "AIDACKCEVSQ6C2EXAMPLE",
6      "arn": "arn:aws:iam::111111111111:user/WMSDK",
7      "accountId": "111111111111",
8      "accessKeyId": "AKIAIOSFODNN7EXAMPLE"
```

```
9      "userName": "WMSDK"
10   },
11   "eventTime": "2017-12-12T17:49:59Z",
12   "eventSource": "workmail.amazonaws.com",
13   "eventName": "CreateUser",
14   "awsRegion": "us-west-2",
15   "sourceIPAddress": "203.0.113.12",
16   "userAgent": "aws-sdk-java/1.11.205 Mac_OS_X/10.11.6 Java_HotSpot(TM)_64-Bit_Server_VM/25.151-
          b12 java/1.8.0_151",
17   "requestParameters": {
18     "name": "janedoe",
19     "displayName": "Jane Doe",
20     "organizationId": "m-5b1c980000EXAMPLE"
21   },
22   "responseElements": {
23     "userId": "a3a9176d-EXAMPLE"
24   },
25   "requestID": "dec81e4a-EXAMPLE",
26   "eventID": "9f2f09c5-EXAMPLE",
27   "eventType": "AwsApiCall",
28   "recipientAccountId": "111111111111"
29 }
```

The following example shows a CloudTrail log entry that demonstrates the CreateAlias action.

```
1  {
2    "eventVersion": "1.05",
3    "userIdentity": {
4      "type": "IAMUser",
5      "principalId": "AIDACKCEVSQ6C2EXAMPLE",
6      "arn": "arn:aws:iam::111111111111:user/WMSDK",
7      "accountId": "111111111111",
8      "accessKeyId": "AKIAIOSFODNN7EXAMPLE",
9      "userName": "WMSDK"
10   },
11   "eventTime": "2017-12-12T18:13:44Z",
12   "eventSource": "workmail.amazonaws.com",
13   "eventName": "CreateAlias",
14   "awsRegion": "us-west-2",
15   "sourceIPAddress": "203.0.113.12",
16   "userAgent": "aws-sdk-java/1.11.205 Mac_OS_X/10.11.6 Java_HotSpot(TM)_64-Bit_Server_VM/25.151-
          b12 java/1.8.0_151",
17   "requestParameters": {
18     "alias": "aliasjamesdoe@testofconsole.awsapps.com",
19     "organizationId": "m-5b1c980000EXAMPLE"
20     "entityId": "a3a9176d-EXAMPLE"
21   },
22   "responseElements": null,
23   "requestID": "dec81e4a-EXAMPLE",
24   "eventID": "9f2f09c5-EXAMPLE",
25   "eventType": "AwsApiCall",
26   "recipientAccountId": "111111111111"
27 }
```

Document History

The following table describes the important changes to the Amazon WorkMail Administrator Guide.

Change	Description	Release Date
Mailbox permissions	You can use mailbox permissions in Amazon WorkMail to grant users or groups the right to work in other users' mailboxes. For more information, see Working with Mailbox Permissions.	April 9, 2018
Support for AWS CloudTrail	Amazon WorkMail is integrated with AWS CloudTrail. For more information, see Logging Amazon WorkMail API Calls with AWS CloudTrail.	December 12, 2017
Support for email flows	You can set up email flow rules for handling incoming email based on a sender's email address or domain. For more information, see Managing Email Flows.	July 5, 2017
Updates to the Quick setup	The Quick setup now creates an Amazon WorkMail directory for you. For more information, see Set up Amazon WorkMail with Quick Setup.	May 10, 2017
Support for a wider range of email clients	You can now use Amazon WorkMail with Microsoft Outlook 2016 for Mac and IMAP email clients. For more information, see Accessing Amazon WorkMail.	January 9, 2017
Support for SMTP journaling	You can set up journaling to record your email communication. For more information, see Using Email Journaling with Amazon WorkMail.	November 25, 2016
Support for email redirection to external email addresses	You can set up email redirection rules by updating the Amazon SES identity policy for your domain. For more information, see Edit Domain Identity Policies.	October 26, 2016
Support for interoperability	You can enable interoperability between Amazon WorkMail and Microsoft Exchange. For more information, see Interoperability Between Amazon WorkMail and Microsoft Exchange.	October 25, 2016
General Availability	The general availability release of Amazon WorkMail.	January 4, 2016

Change	Description	Release Date
Support for reserving resources	Support for reserving resources, such as meeting rooms and equipment. For more information, see Working with Resources.	October 19, 2015
Support for the email migration tool	Support for the email migration tool. For more information, see Migrating to Amazon WorkMail.	August 16, 2015
Preview	The preview release of Amazon WorkMail.	January 28, 2015

www.ingramcontent.com/pod-product-compliance
Lightning Source LLC
LaVergne TN
LVHW082041050326
832904LV00005B/263